WHAT YOU
SHOULD KNOW?
THAT YOUR PARENTS WERE
CLUELESS ABOUT

SHADI RAZAVIAN

First Published in November 2021

ISBN: 978-93-5472-692-7

BLUEROSE PUBLISHERS
www.bluerosepublishers.com
info@bluerosepublishers.com
+91 8882 898 898

Cover Design:
Niloufar Razavian

Typographic Design:
Ilma Mirza

Distributed by: BlueRose, Amazon, Flipkart

I dedicate this book to my beautiful mother

and all those mothers who didn't know any better

And

Also to my amazing daughter Niloufar

and all the young ladies who will someday be mothers

and "Now know better"

WORDS OF GRATITUDE

I am eternally grateful to my parents because I know they did the best they could and I love them deeply . I can not miss mentioning my sister in my gratitude list, she is and always has been my hero , someone I looked up to growing up and I have deep respect and love for, as an adult .

My daughter who is my heart out side of me . She is the sole reason I want to be the better version of me every day .

My son who taught me the real meaning of forgiveness.

My life partner who loves me with all my weirdness and is my true soul mate.

And countless mentors who have been instrumental in all my growth , the list is long and my gratitude , infinite.

Last not the least , to Pete Cohan for being gracious and writing the foreword to this book. I got to know him and his amazing work through social media and later had the opportunity to connect with him . A man who believes , together we can achieve more. And begins his talks with Happy Beautiful day.

He genuinely contributes to many people's beautiful days across the globe. No words can express my gratitude.

Foreword

"I was absolutely delighted to be asked to write the forward for this book.

 What Shadi has created in this book is truly an inspiration regarding the impact that words have on us and how we have the opportunity with our words to massively transform not only our lives but of the lives of people around us.

We need to wake up to the reality that children are born confident but it's the programming they are exposed to that shapes their world.

Shadi carefully lays out what we can do to create positive change with the words that we use to empower parents to have more impact on their children

I would highly recommend this book it's beautiful

Pete Cohen

British Speaker ,

Author /podcaster

Executive Coach/Wellbeing Expert

Table of Content

Prelude

I can still hear some of the words in my head. The words that meant so little for them as they said it but it just seems to have gone right through my senses into my brain and made a permanent home there.

Growing up, I always wondered why all the adults spoke about their children in the third person.

"She never drinks her milk!"

"She doesn't wake up on time for school ever!"

"She has been troubling me for studying!"

On and on……

I always felt like saying: "Hellllooooooo big people I am present in the room and can hear you very well."

This is not even as important as the part that adults love to tell us Who we are as kids

"You are too lazy!"

"You can't be this stupid, how could you do that?"!!!!!

"Don't be greedy!"

"Don't be clumsy!"

Tagging is what this is called in psychology and I have learned that now after years of studying, researching, learning and God knows hours of working on my own mind.

Adults bring a child into this world and are obliged to take care of that little helpless (physically) being.

What they don't get is that they are part of the process of programming the mind of that child. They are completely oblivious to the importance of EVERY word they utter. They have no clue of the fact that a baby is born with a clean slate with just a few innate characteristics. She/He just knows:

1. I am amazing
2. I can ask for anything and I will get it
3. I am lovable
4. I must survive

Shocked!!!!!

Yes, it is the truth. We are born with this huge self-confidence and a cent per cent belief that we are adorable. We are lovable and perfect.

CHAPTER 1

ASK THE QUESTION

Then what happens along the way!!!!!

Why does a 6 year -old sits on the stairs and cries and if asked she will reply: "My mom doesn't love me "!

I am coming back to this again. Let me share some of my stories.

Did I always know that my mother loves me even though she said things that made me feel so "not significant"!!!! As a child, I tried hard to make myself believe that the words had nothing to do with her love. A mighty task for a child, Since as kids we believe what we see and hear. At first, a child doesn't have previous experience. It is only with repeated incidents of what she hears or sees that she believes and this Belief is going right to the archives of her subconscious where it gets stored forever, or until she decides to change it.

Back to my story...

That even though time and again, she would say right in front of a group of friends or acquaintances "She also writes stories." You must be wondering that is not a bad thing to say but for me, it was because I DIDN'T write stories as a child. Just because my sister wrote poetry everyone assumed I was also supposed to be another genius of the family and the worst was, her lame attempts to save face by coming up with" she writes stories " ....

Ohhh it was difficult to reassure me that she truly loved me as much as my sister.

She didn't know the damage that she was doing, I know that today, but that 9 years old wondered "Why is my mother lying about me???" as a child, I kept thinking that what I truly was, was Not ENOUGH for her so she had to make up something to tell others I was good at, that something which I was clueless about.

This was the beginning of my I AM NOT ENOUGH journey.

I know it now. I see it now and I recognize it now.

When she told me the story of how she loved me as a baby because I was so chubby and cute! It all sounds so simple and innocent and yet today I know all my life I stayed "chubby" so that she would love me. You see, a child's mind is very simple, it connects the dots as presented to it. I also am aware some of you would think to yourself "Yes blame your shortcomings on your mother, good way out." But you see as I mentioned before, We are born feeling perfect and the only reason for this change is all that we hear from people we find primarily important.

I had done my math in my head. She doesn't think I am enough since she makes up lies about who I am, and she says she loved me when I was born because I was chubby. It didn't take a genius to decide "if I am chubby she will always love me!!!"

I struggled with my weight all my adolescence and much later until I knew better.

And of course, there is the Good Girl tag with which I lived most of my life and I take that tag as the curse of my life. Let me explain why

I was always the Good girl of the family. Looking back I don't even know how I got there. Probably my mind decided very early in life that if I couldn't be the genius of the family whom she brags about I had to be something else. Since I anyways didn't feel significant to show off "What I Actually was good at ", in that case, might as well just follow along and be the Good Girl.

No complaints, No opinions, Great grades, basically live in the shadow of those who mattered.

Yup, the good girl crown had to come to yours truly every year so I kept on being the one that never has an existence since that was the way I had learnt to receive the crown.

Tagging Tagging .....That's why I hate tagging now.

My intention here to share is not because I am in anyways holding on to these against my mother NO. To your surprise, I managed to have quite a close and amicable relationship with her later in life. I stopped blaming her long before I completely understood how our mind works. However, after knowing about the programming we all go through I knew much better than ever to hold a grudge against the one and only one I knew genuinely loved me. She was the victim of her own programming. That was a great relief.

 I simply believe there will be so many of you (readers) who will see your own life experiences in mine. I want everyone to recognize the signs.

I have a step by step system that has worked beautifully for me and love to share it with my clients.

1. Recognize
2. Acknowledge
3. Accept
4. Let it go

And it has worked for me.

I grew up to believe the way to be significant was through academic performance. I was an A+ student, a good girl (as mentioned before). Today as I look back I see this little girl who all she needed was to feel significant.

My mother didn't even realize those few words, the lies about what I was good at had changed my perception of me forever or at least for most of my life.

The race to matter in her eyes was one with no final destination. Because I was never going to be good at what she felt, worthy of significance. I decided I wasn't good enough for her. And concluded,

I was not good enough......

You see the problem with "I am not good enough" is your mind does not distinguish if you are not good enough for this or for that. Your stubborn mind (which has a mind of its own) just generalizes and with almost a permanent finality concludes "I am not good enough"

Going back to my story...

When my mother had to praise me it was always about the "good girl " I was, or even worse, how I kept everyone ahead of myself. She would proudly narrate:" This girl always waits to see everyone has eaten and if there is something left she will pick up."

Today as a mother I am amazed why would a mother encourage her child to be Self-Sacrificial ?!!

I know she was looking for something nice to say about me. She thought that was the way to praise. Little did she know that she had set the ball rolling for a girl who never asked for what she desires in life ......it was only recently that I learned how to ask for help, ask for what I need or what I desire. I lived putting everyone on a higher pedestal, believing I was to give, give and give more without ever receiving ...

Mind you I am still a giver, and I believe if you give more, you will receive more ... but you see I am no more the self–sacrificing girl I used to be then. Today I give because it brings me immense pleasure to see someone happily receiving what I have to offer. Be it a gift, my time or my knowledge.

What mistakes we make when we use words, sentences that seem so simple and unimportant to us and yet they go on to be building blocks for another's lifetime of pain and despair.

Words can make or break us.

For a reason unknown to me I never ever held my sister responsible for how I felt. I am so grateful for that because I grew up to love her and respect her for everything she has been to me. Growing up, I was in awe of her. I still am.

But once again, it was my mother who proudly told everyone:" She never asks me for anything, she goes to her elder sister ".

I am a mother today and I can't begin to understand in which world that is a good thing !!! The fact that I had no connection with my own mother? The fact that I had realized my voice will not be heard by the most significant person in my world?

So harmless to many and so deeply life-changing to a child.....

Alright, I think I have made my point by now. I can come up with so many other instances, words and sentences that my mind hung onto. The words that became the solid foundation to the person I grew up to become. The words that became the reason I treated myself with an unkind, uncompromising manner, and most importantly words that became the pillars of my relationships as an adult.

It wasn't easy to recognize why my relationships were the way they were, it wasn't easy to realize where the root cause of all my lack of self-esteem, self-image and self-worth was coming from. It took years of seeking, working on myself, learning and reading, even self-hypnosis to see it all so clearly and complete my first stage Recognize.

We keep wondering why do We get into relationships where We are not respected, why can't

We say what We want, why don't We have the strength to stand up for what's important to us, why can't We do all that We desire to do or even worse why don't We feel Love for ourselves???

So many questions and the worst part is that many of us don't even get to the stage of questioning all this. We remain in the miserable state of "I am Not good enough" and never really know it. We blame everyone for not doing something for us or to us or not being there for us at the time we most needed them, and yet we don't really recognize the words that made us feel the way we do today. The words that are so engraved within our programming that we most probably even use for ourselves. They are the adjectives or descriptions we have for ourselves. But we fail to see where did they actually come from?

Do you think one day you wake up and decide you are a clumsy person? Or that you are no good at something? Whenever I did ask someone who says:" I am not good at Math ", why do you say so? The reply is normally "I just am not" little that person knows that somewhere along the way perhaps in the 3rd or 4th grade a teacher must have told him "you are not good at Math, " and there it is the first blow ... a seed of doubt already sown "I can't do Numbers " with the doubt already in place, confidence shaky, year after year he just gets worse at numbers because each time he sees a math problem his subconscious is reminded "You are not good at Math"

And did the teacher know how deep those words can cut??? Almost surely not.

We find partners whose attitude and behaviours resemble the very person we dreaded or loved most while growing! And why do you think that is? The words that we heard from the significant person in our lives the very first 5 years of our lives carved the belief. The belief of how we should be treated, with respect and love or like an insignificant person whose voice is not to be heard.

As human beings, we tend to take most things in life for granted. Our health, Our relationships, Our wealth and even Our very own words.

How many times have you been in a situation where someone said something and then followed it with "I didn't mean it that way!" But it is not what was meant that matters, it is the invisible effect that those syllables have on our subconscious that matters.

We have read so many quotes about the power of our words.

"Be careful with your words. Once they are said, they can be only forgiven, not forgotten."

These were many wise men who knew the value of every word that is uttered.

Once you recognize the beliefs that are holding you back and limiting your very existence, you need to Acknowledge that. Why so, you ask? Because unless and until we acknowledge that there are beliefs that don't serve us well, words that are not even OURS. Beliefs that have been fed to us probably decades before, even before we knew who we really are and what's our reality in this world, We cannot move to the next step of Acceptance.

 Now the strange part of how our mind works is that we love the familiar even if it is not the most constructive and lucrative for us. We hold on to what we know as truth and obviously what has been fed to us as innocent children. I am talking about words from our most trusted caregivers or teachers all of whom we adore as kids. Their every word will always seem like the "   The God- honest Truth ". The commandments, Words we hang on to like anchors. These words are the foundation of all the core values we gradually hold dear to us.

So acknowledging something that we are so familiar with, as a destructive and limiting belief is not a simple act. The truth is, it probably is a process for most of us. One that almost surely we need help with.

I made this journey all on my own and it wasn't easy. Yet, I am here sharing all this because I know in my heart this can be most helpful to so many of you dear readers.

Once we acknowledge this truth only then can we Accept. You must be wondering, what is there to accept? Accept that you have found the reason for all your miseries and that you now know for sure where to look to make decisions that are enriching and empowering. Accept that no one but yourself can help you. Acceptance is a huge part of any healing process. As I said before, it is essential that you recognize and acknowledge that you indeed are not your best self and in desperate need of " Healing your Soul ". The acceptance, that you are much greater than you were made to believe. The acceptance, that until now you lived the beliefs, thoughts, opinions and words of others, who though meant well for you, didn't necessarily know any better themselves.

You see, I am definitely not on a crusade to make every one of you hate your parents or teachers. I just want us to know if life is not how we want it to be, we have been fed the wrong program. And at this stage, once we recognize, acknowledge and accept, the mere understanding of the cause of our problems is one hell of an empowering experience.

You accept that simple fact that:

I am infinitely powerful and born with immense self-confidence.

I can change all of the programmings in my subconscious if I decide.

I am the creator of my own life.

I can reprogram my mind (subconscious) in a way that it works in my favour and only for me and not against me.

I, now acknowledge and accept that it was all the limiting and destructive programming that was holding me back from being the best version of myself.

I, now feel liberated and in charge of my own mind and my own life.

I, now know the power of my words and use only words that make me the best version of myself.

I am now taking full responsibility for the programming of my subconscious mind.

I am empowered.

I am worthy.

I am enough.

Before getting to the last stage, you will need to be patient and kind to yourself and it will surely take some time for you to get fully convinced of the acknowledgements you are making to yourself.

After this stage, all you do is Let go of the old limiting programs which your parents, relatives, teachers, peers, the society so lovingly and with full concern dumped on you.

It is constant work. Yes, You can't expect yourself to magically never ever again go back to that old wiring, We will talk about how it is absolutely crucial to replace that useless programming with one that works for you, but it is so liberating instantly that you never want to be back in that old space of doubt and I am Not enough.

CHAPTER 2

MIND YOUR WORDS BECAUSE WORDS ARE CREATIVE

Some of you might wonder why have I gone into all the explanations when the book titles "what you must know that your parents didn't!"

That is because being a parent is one of the biggest responsibilities of any person's life. It is a lifetime commitment. It is about being the reason for another being's existence. It is about the future. The next generation of the society. It is by no means a topic to be taken lightly.

Unless we heal our own minds and totally understand how the words of our own parents have made us the people we are today, we are never going to see value in what we need to do when it comes to our own child!

We forget the power of our words especially when it comes to our children. The irony is that as kids we all have been undermined at one time or other by our parents or adults around us, when we felt so hurt with the words we heard and yet as we become adults and hold the power of words over the young ones in our lives, very conveniently we forget how it felt to be on the other side of this equation.

If we truly understand and recognize the power of our words, probably we would begin to appreciate silence much more.

I have always wondered about those who constantly talk. I believe every word is like a pearl that is precious and can bring immense happiness to the receiver of it. Or, it is a dagger that can tear the receiver's heart apart.

"Handle them carefully, for words have more power than atom bombs." -Pearl Strachan Hurd

We learn the sounds of words much before learning their meanings. A child only understands the meaning of a chair after seeing one and sitting on it. The connection between the sounds and their meaning is taught to us in school and before that by our parents.

"This is a doll" the child holds it and she repeats "doll".

What we don't teach our kids or perhaps no one ever taught us is that every sound has its own energy.

Why is it that sometimes or the other in your life you might have been in a situation where you say" I just didn't like the way he said those words"

Probably the words were quite mundane routine ones but what made you cringe was the energy behind the words. Have you ever been in that place? Have you given it much thought? Now is the time.

What we don't learn is the energetic effect of these words. How they not only express literal meaning, also an inner meaning which goes right through the hearts of the listener.

I believe the major issue here is not that we don't know how hurtful our words can be if used thoughtlessly. What No one teaches us is that these words are so strong that they can create new neuro-pathways in the brain. You ask what does that mean? That means it can alter the way we do things, it can change the way we see ourselves, it can make us believe things that most probably are not remotely true about ourselves or the world. These words can be the foundation of a very strong and able personality or one with major dysfunctional issues.

The lasting effect of each word we use cannot be dismissed.

Yes, they flow freely but do they cost us heavily ohhhh boy.

"Words are free. It's how you use them that may cost you."

–KushandWizdom

Words can cost us our relationships not only temporarily but forever. You say the wrong thing and then you have a huge argument. You scream and shout at each other, say the worst and don't talk to the person for days, weeks sometimes years. This is bad enough, isn't it? This is the cost of the lack of self-awareness.

I know we all have moments where we lose our control and say stuff we don't really mean but the issue is even when the speaker would conveniently forget what he said in a moment of rage, The receiver will almost never. That is the impact of our words.

Like they say: "Words are more powerful than a weapon"

And the icing on the cake is that our words can affect people we care for, the ones we love more than life itself. What you say to your partner can stop him or her from chasing their dreams.

You probably feel "I just told her how I feel about the situation, I am practical. " but what you said simply sent the message "YOU CANNOT DO ANYTHING RIGHT"

I got married really young to a man who was a narcissist. keeping that aside as a young partner what I wanted most was support and some encouraging words which not only I never received, I was constantly reminded of how not good enough I was.

What do you think that did to my self-esteem? I agree some would say how could you allow someone's words to have such an impact on how you perceive yourself! You see, this is all happening subconsciously. The same way we never understood our parents' comments can define what career we choose??

Today I disclose everything I have learnt and understood of my own life because it is no more so complicated. Once deciphered, it all makes sense.

And all those years of helplessness seem futile but then I didn't know I could change the programming which was being loaded on my personal computer through Repetition.

"What's repeated will be your point of focus and what you focus on, you will be"

Now I know so many will read this and say what the **** .does it mean we can't just be saying what we think freely? Without having to evaluate it???

My answer to that is if you really understand what my message is in this book, If you truly understand the importance of every word that you utter and its effects on the other person, you will naturally and spontaneously begin to speak in such a manner which is only empowering ....

"Your words have power. Speak words that are kind, loving, positive, uplifting, encouraging, and life-giving." - Unknown

I believe in strengthening the foundations of a building and in our society, the foundation is our children. If as parents we have the awareness and the wisdom to speak the right way to our children and use the words that only empower them imagine how much better off our society would grow to be. Generations can improve in how they see themselves. A generation that has the highest self-esteem can achieve anything it sets its mind on.

Once I began to notice and recollect the words that I had heard so often from people who mattered to me and even those that didn't, I could see the ripple effects of each.

How they influenced the person I became and my relationship with myself and everyone whom I came across with.

I had read somewhere years ago that '"Thoughts are creative" today I understand the meaning of that sentence so clearly.

Every thought is initiated with words we tell ourselves or we use, and the power of these words to create our world.

Imagine basing your thoughts on the words you hear from others, ones that are not so constructive or even true. Checking our frequently used words lead us to our dominant thoughts.

1. Make a list of the words you use most frequently each day
2. Separate the positive and negative
3. Evaluate which ones are more
4. Introspect on the effect of these negative words
5. How do they make you feel?
6. Find the chain of thought that they create in your mind

Let's set an intention to stop using these words

Attempt and see the change in your attitude and daily life.

CHAPTER 3

TOUGH JOB OF BEING A PARENT

As parents we have been on the other side of the fence .yes we were little people at the mercy of the big people. Bombarded with their words, words that came like fireballs out of a cannon and destroyed the structure, that structure which was how we saw ourselves.

Our self-esteem.

The strange part is that we are oblivious to this truth."Our words get engraved into the subconscious mind." Be it ours or the little being we are responsible for.

A child steps into this world from the comfort of the cocoon that he knows for nine months. It is like returning from a vacation on the beaches of the Bahamas. All the heat, comfort, soft sand loads of great fluids to enjoy. Now all of a sudden reality hits, it is cold and huge, this world. That little being has one concern "How do I survive? Who is going to feed me and keep me warm!!!"?

The fortunate ones have a loving mother and a protective father to take care of the child's first and primary need SAFETY. But that's not all. It has been proven that infants who don't receive their mother's love at birth, especially for the first few months have lesser chances of survival.

And why do we think that is? Love is the antidote for so many things in life, isn't it? For a baby, love becomes the reason to live. A child's first lesson of life is Love. To be loved and to Love.

A baby knows he is adorable and deserves all the love and attention in the world. That's why he doesn't care if he has to eat or poop in the oddest hour of the night! He just does what he feels like and he believes in the depth of his heart that someone must serve him all that he desires That's the level of self-confidence we all are born with. All we know is we are lovable and deserving of love. But, The big But .....

But somewhere as we grow up, this changes. Somewhere between the age of 3 and 7 we revisit these natural beliefs and begin to wonder if we are worthy of love? Can we ask for everything we desire? Will I get what I want if I ask the adult?

It is such an ironic matter. Because as new parents when your baby cries for food or sleep or God alone knows what else we jump and run around and try to find a way to pacify the baby (or at least most decent parents do this) but as the child grows into a toddler and grows up, gradually and very convincingly for the good of the child we stop bouncing for every need of his. And then somewhere along the way we decide enough is enough He or She can't get everything.

Now I know at this very paragraph many of you think "ok how can we always say yes to our child? Will we not bring narcissists into this world ?? point taken .. but allow me to explain

Yes, every child has to learn to hear the word NO. This is essential for a healthy mental balance and mostly for future adjustments in a world where there is way too much negation.

But unfortunately, our focus remains on the primary needs of the child more and more. Food, clothing, shelter and education, all and every need of the child !! what we begin to overlook is the need for healthy self-esteem and that is directly dependent on how you teach them the word NO.

Research has shown that an average teenager has heard the word NO more than 145000 times already !!! Can you believe that? I was criticized by many for the same statement. However, I refuse to back off. It is all about how you teach your child that he has to know the word NO! That at times in life we might not be able to get what we desire BUT and this is the huge BUT

BUT we must make sure our child understands that if you don't get something right now, and if what he or she desires is not dangerous or harmful to himself or the world around him, he need not give up the hope of getting it someday. Do I make sense?

There is No and then there is No !!! A NO that is finite and says you don't get this because you are insignificant (there we go back to basic needs) and then there is a No which says for these reasons you won't get what you desire NOW but for all probability if you keep at it you won't be disappointed.

I know for many of my readers I seem to be an idealist and believe it or not I am proud to say despite all the raw deals Life has dealt me I am an idealist because I truly believe in the Power that We Are.

Creators of our own destiny.

Just if we are clear about how it all works in our mind.

All I want to bring to light is how to create a generation of adults who believe in themselves? People who don't give up, or shy away from asking in fear of rejection.

Children learn rejection very early on through the constant negative words of their primary caretakers. "The almighty Parents"

When we abruptly finish a conversation with a child with the word " NO" ! all that a suggestible subconscious mind has understood is that "I can't ask because I won't get!" "Because I am not significant, not enough!"

Isn't that what many of us think even today as adults?

How many of us don't ask for anything of ourselves or others because we have a limiting belief that "I won't get it, why ask?"

"No, because I said so and I am your mother/father". How many of us have heard this sentence while growing up? Being a parent is not a given authority or an open license to destroying your child's sense of significance. Just because we bring a child into this world (mind you the creation is not ours even) so many of us think we can and must have control over the little being who is called "my son/daughter" the possessive adjectives that seem to give the right to us to abuse and manipulate and control!!!!

I repeat, parents don't wake up and decide to overpower or abuse their children or most of them don't who own healthy mental status, however, unless we learn the effects of how we treat or speak to our kids there is no way we can correct what was done wrong to us.

I know some parents won't like what they read here and I reassure them I am a mother and I have made mistakes as a parent but I also recognize those and see the need of the hour to create an awareness for all parents to see the effect their every word can have, on the kind of an adult their child will grow up to be. Even in the kind of husband or wife, they will be and most importantly the kind of parents they will be to the next generation.

We feel responsible for our child's daily routine. We know that it is our job to feed and dress our kids. Make sure they get the right education. We are almost obsessed with discipline.

Well, all of these apply to most decent parents, right?

We always think we know what's right for our kids and in this knowing, we end up doing some great damage along the way. I had read somewhere that "A child doesn't learn from what you say but from what you do!"

I have dwelled upon this for years and whilst I understand the value of the statement I also believe it is a bit overrated. Let me explain my thoughts

Yes, your child is a sponge. Taking in every bit of what happens around. I still remember when my daughter was barely 3 years old and had just begun pre-school. One day I went to pick her up and her teacher told me with a huge smile how my princess had narrated the entire weekend's events to her all to the gory details. What an embarrassment!

But that is exactly what kids do. They remember every event, every action. This is merely out of their complete adoration for their parents and of course the fantastic memory that they all seem to be blessed with until they reach teenage years.

Yes, It is true. Your kid is watching every action of yours to the smallest detail. So watch how you eat, how you dress and how you react to your people. Heck, you got to be careful when you want to scratch your private parts while sitting in your living room because those little eyes are not missing a move.

But more importantly, watch what you say when you are happy or sad or frustrated. This we all know and not to mention yet so many parents undermine this fact. Your child is modeling after you.

While I was managing a Child Care Center, It was fascinating for me to see some of the behaviour patterns of my kids' actions. Actions and more importantly words that were undoubtedly not natural to a child. And where do you think they were picking up those from?

I usually had to call in the parents and as tactfully as possible let them know that they had to watch their actions at home. They had to be reminded of the little being who is always watching even when he or she seems busy somewhere else.

However, what we don't pay much attention to is, not only that little person is watching, he/she is also listening very very keenly. So, of course of the kind of conversations that floated in their home environment.

How many times have you heard a child repeat a sentence right from their parent's conversation? At times even the self-talk. As I mentioned I was working with little kids for years. I would hear the girls having self-talk like "I am not looking nice today!!!" or "I am looking fat in this dress!!!!"

And where do you think a 6 year -old would get that from? This is the recording of her mother's self-talk or probably a conversation she has had with her husband.

In today's social media-obsessed world, we see so many encouraging their tiny little kids to imitate a typical adult behaviour merely to get more views and likes. It saddens me to see how unaware and oblivious to the consequences of such actions they are.

Over the years I have caught myself talking exactly like my own mother. Ironic, isn't it? Even after all these years what I heard as a child is still recorded and replays from time to time. With one simple difference, now I live with the awareness that guides me to edit and correct my unwanted recorded programming. Just as quickly as it comes out of my mouth.

It is funny how I find myself saying things to my daughter and then realize that I sounded exactly like my own mom. That's the power of words and the ability of the subconscious mind to record and replay all that is recorded.

Yes at times, it is not life-changing but take it from me almost every word has an impact on who we see ourselves, how we see ourselves and even our world.

Now that your child is listening to everything all the time let's consider if what we say to ourselves has an impact on our child, imagine the impact of what you say directly to your child????!!!!

When she has not cleaned her room and you call her "messy"

When he has come home with a scratch on his knees and you call him "clumsy"

When she has not received the grades you hoped for because of some silly mistake and you call her "stupid"

When you found your son watching TV for longer than he was allowed and you call him "couch potato"

All these instances don't seem much, isn't it? In some households using such name-calling or probably even more harsh words are quite the way of life. A routine business. Nothing alarming.

What as parents we MUST know and get educated about is Just how effective every single one of these adjectives is in the way your child feels about him or herself.

The child that has been called clumsy will grow to believe He is in fact clumsy and can't do anything right. Do you know why? Because he has heard this often enough to take it as The Truth engraved on his subconscious and programmed to be a clumsy one. So you are proven absolutely correct. He is a clumsy adult.

Every child is born with a conscious and subconscious mind as clean as purest holy waters. They know nothing but that they are born as amazing and perfect beings. They only know themselves so they believe they are lovable.

As they say " We are born in the image of the creator"

Pure and perfect.

Once they step into this world, it is the mother and father and gradually people around them that begin writing on the clean slate of their subconscious.

That is as graphically as I can possibly describe to you, dear reader, the importance of your every word in creating a child who goes on to believe he can conquer the world or one who hides away from every opportunity in life because someone along the way told him things that he concluded "I am not good enough, I can't do this"

We become who we are not only from our inherent traits but more so from all the experiences that we go through in the course of our life. .

These experiences are dominantly connected to what people in our lives have told us.

I still can't get an incident that happened more than four decades ago, out of my mind. The words that were said about me by a little boy I liked when I was barely 6 years old. He called me a "fat girl". I was always a chubby child, even when I was born. My mother's greatest joy was to tell the story about how happy she was when I was born because I looked like a white fluff ball. She expressed she loved me so much instantly because I was a chubby baby. Incidentally, my elder sister was born really small and thin. And I was so round and she fell in love with me.

Alas, she didn't know she had with a few words of well-intended adoration, set me to a lifetime of struggle with my weight. A lifetime of unhappiness with my body.

It all seems impossible to believe to most of you, I know that but believe it or not, it took me 4 decades and many self-hypnosis sessions to recognize the root cause of my unhappiness with my own body.

Her words had programmed my subconscious to connect being loved with being overweight and I couldn't let the weight go. Not because I ate too much or due to bad lifestyle. It simply was the program I lived with for so many years of my life. Thanks to the one person who loved me most.

Not intentional, definitely not. But ignorant! surely yes .....

CHAPTER 4

WHAT YOU SHOULD KNOW IS…

I am passionate about the use of my words. I have been on both ends. As a child to an ignorant mom and as an ignorant mother to a child.

Today, I am grateful for the awareness that I have gained and I want to share this with everyone who cares to listen and in this process I am open to self-disclosure.

I believe we are the sum total of all our beliefs. Some call it "The Paradigm". This is a series of fixated thoughts and opinions that we don't seem to let go of. But after years, I also realized that we can achieve a level of self-realization which helps us to have a paradigm (belief system) that is building us up and not tearing us down.

Our mind has a few simple rules and as soon as I understood these I knew my life will never be the same. Once you know how you can master the mind, the transformation begins instantly.

It is simple, Your mind loves the familiar. At this stage, I have a bad and a good news for all of you. Yes familiar is what your mind craves for and unfortunately for almost all of us we seem to have many negative practices like self-criticism and self-doubt, self-sabotaging behaviour which of course we got very familiar with thanks to our primary and first caregivers.

Do you know why we prefer to criticize ourselves instead of praise?

This is because very early in life very significant people who we look up to, tell us that it is NOT OK to self- praise. They teach us modesty which I agree is a virtue .what they do not explain to us is the difference between modesty and self-demeaning behaviour!

We are taught to be humble and not arrogant about what we are good at. They tell us not to sing our own praise or blow our own trumpet, what they fail to explain is that having self-worth and arrogance is not the same.

Just because I know what I can do or what I am great at doesn't make me an arrogant person. I do not have to rub it in everyone's face, yes true, but at the same time unless I say what I am good at, how in God's name anyone would know about it !!!?

When you go for a job interview and you are expected to talk about your skills or strengths, while all your life you have been taught that talking about yourself is not Ok! How in God's name are you suppose to be confident and speak with pride (not arrogance)?

This is why I say, our culture and society doesn't prepare us for success. This is why successful people are way lesser in number than unsuccessful ones. How many have been brought up by parents who set them for success and winning?

I know of people who have grown up, being reminded repeatedly of the fact that "You are not perfect" instead of "You are your better version every day"

The fact that we are told to find faults with ourselves has made us highly self-critical even if it is in the silliest and most minor situations.

How many of us say things like "I am so stupid, I am so clumsy, I always mess things up, I have no luck and so on and on.....

I am sure it all seems familiar, doesn't it?

The parental compulsive attitude to teach high morals to their child can get distorted easily if the parent does not possess the understanding of how our mind works and the extent of the word influence on the subconscious mind. This is why I have been dedicating my time to bring as much awareness as I can amongst as many parents.

We are taught self-criticism by repeatedly being reminded to first check our own faults and mistakes. This is an innocent attempt to keep us grounded and humble. The problem is this is going to backfire in life if we are not guided through a healthy approach to criticism.

Whether it is self-induced or from outside sources, a criticism can have positive or absolutely destructive results.

Most of us grow with a fear of rejection or disapproval. Add to this a fear of failure and the concoction is perfect for a person with less than zero self-worth and self-image.

I like to put in the process of a healthy approach to criticism here. This is an invaluable share and I hope can be duly noted by all.

Let's say,

A message of self-criticism or someone's critical point of view of you or your actions has been received.

Most of us react in two possible ways

First Scenario: Anger, and counter blame fueled with "I don't give a damn"

Second Scenario: upset, sadness, self-deprecating thoughts and self-blame and the cherry on the top is "I AM NOT ENOUGH" which I like to call a disease.

Can you see the pictures I am trying to create in your mind's vision? How many times have you been in such situations? Maybe the first or second Scenario? Sometimes this and other times that?

You see, Criticism is a crucial element in progress for all of us. It helps us to consider points to improve. It shows us that we are never perfect and we can be our own improved version at each step. Alas, only if we knew how to process it in a way that it lights our path and not throw us in the dungeons of self-defeat and self-pity while putting others on the pedestal of grandiosity!

Here is the way I believe that criticism can be processed healthily

1. Once fault or mistake brought to your attention. Pause and breathe
2. Consider how close to facts these criticisms are by having a logical argument with your own self. This happens by you looking for facts and evidence that either supports or dismisses the accusation (sclf or otherwise)
3. At this junction, if there is truth to the criticism
4. Find steps for self-correction while acknowledging and accepting your shortcoming WITHOUT hovering on self-blame or self-deprecation
5. If the facts only prove that there never existed any basis to the criticism (self or otherwise) All

you do is to LET IT GO without pointing a finger at the critic (your or someone else)

The truth is we are wired to love ourselves. The baby simply loves his own body that's why you find babies sucking at their own toes or staring at their own image in the mirror. However, our society tells us differently and shames us for this self-love as we grow up, hence the journey of self-criticism.

Changing our response to criticism can be another empowering step towards finding that self-love with which we were created.

And as we grow older and if we are fortunate enough we realize that almost all the reasons for unhappiness in our lives is our lack of self-love. Then we will go around finding people like me and books like this, struggling to get back on that flight of selfishness.

There, I do it again. You ask SELFISHNESS but isn't that a terrible thing? To be selfish?!!

I recently got a perfect definition for the word selfish: "One that is in connection with the SELF"

And who is the self? The "Higher consciousness" that we are all the image of.

And why is it bad to be in connection, to be selfish and love oneself enough to be the best version of oneself? The world would be a much happier place if every one of us had so much love for ourselves, so fulfilled with ourselves that we could pour out to every soul around us.

Imagine a place where Love flows. No criticism, No negative words. Only Love.

The issue is our dear mind gets so familiar with this self-critic that it only desires to hear the same and no other voice is heard unless we consciously change this habitual behaviour and make self-praise and positive comments and adjectives familiar to our mind.

The bigger issue is we believe the praise has to come from someone outside of ourselves. Our parents, friends and teachers anyone and everyone we come across with. What we don't know about our mind is that it is clever enough to take everyone else's praises and compliments as something with a motive!!! That is, for our mind the only praise that sticks and is truly accepted is the one that comes from Yourself ☺

So let's make self-praise familiar to our mind instead of self-critical comments day in and out. They all seem so insignificant but the damage each negative word does to your self-worth, self-esteem is beyond belief.

As we said this mind of ours is very clever and has its own rules but once we understand how it works, it is mighty easy to make it work for us.

Words that we use can make or break the listener, be it yourself or your child. A lot has been said about how we should talk to ourselves ....

What we must be reminded constantly of is

What we should "NOT " say to our children.

CHAPTER 5

UNDERSTAND THE POWER OF YOUR WORDS AND THEIR ENERGY

We bring a child into this world mainly for our very own pleasure and solely to satisfy our ego. To think of it probably if a child knew how dependent he or she is going to be on the parents who are the means for his or her birth, would not even agree to come into this world.

We decide to have children because our biological clock is ticking or even worse because of the pressure from the people around us, society looks at couples without children as though they have come from Mars. To escape the whispers and nasty comments, the mean gossip, many couples decide to take a huge step into parenthood.

This decision not only changes their own lives forever it also makes them responsible for a new life. An innocent life who has no clue what is awaiting it.

The process of procreation is one that seems to be taken so lightly by most. The level of awareness in to the whole life-changing process is not even close to what it needs to be.

Having said that I am not here to scare you all especially newly married ones who are -I am sure- looking forward to having beautiful little ones. I am a mother of two, have worked with kids of all ages and I sincerely believe having a child is a magical experience. Being the reason for another heart beating, another soul stepping into this world is nothing short of a miracle.

What I like to bring into focus here is all that we need to know even before we take this step. We must know bringing a child into this world is much more than feeding and clothing, sending them to school and keeping them physically safe. What's even more important is the responsibility of keeping their MIND safe, the responsibility of making them not only physically but emotionally independent strong and powerful beings.

For decades and decades, parents thought their job ends by feeding and keeping their children safe providing a safe home and basic amenities. Then came the era of parents getting more aware of the importance of the home -environment. How it would affect their children if they didn't get along and kept fighting. In more forward countries the governments took upon themselves to create organizations that took care of children's wellbeing.

Cases of parental abuse were on the rise, not because it was a new phenomenon but because the awareness had risen. Now, even children knew they had rights, that their parents couldn't physically or mentally abuse them. This was a glorious era for the little innocent beings of the world.

Mind you, even today there are countries, third world and developing like India, where children still are abused day in and out and no one cares or knows or moves forward to help.

This is not exactly why I am writing this book. Yes, we moved into the stage of awareness of how important a child's mental and psychological wellbeing is a couple of decades back, but today we know even more.

Today we know, a child becomes exactly the person he or she hears the parents accuse her of being. A child believes what he or she hears and that becomes his world, his personality.

Today we know the power of words. There are scientific pieces of evidence to back up this claim. children who have heard their parents calling them names, tagging them as stupid, daft, clutz and so many other negative adjectives, grow to be those things. Not because they are born that way but because they were told so many times that they began to believe it and what we believe is who we become.

Here I quote from the book, *Words Can Change Your Brain,* jointly written by Dr. Andrew Newberg, a neuroscientist at Thomas Jefferson University, and Mark Robert Waldman, a communications expert , *"a single word* has the power to influence the expression of genes that regulate physical and emotional stress."

Furthermore, according to these two experts in their field, **exercising positive thoughts can quite literally change one's reality.**

And how do we exercise the positive thoughts by choosing our words deliberately so that we can only emit high vibrating energy.

Doesn't that sound easy? Unfortunately, we believe what's easy does not work.

"If speaking kindly to plants helps them grow, imagine what speaking kindly to people can do?"

There are various studies on how plants respond to loving words and hateful ones. My grandmother had a green thumb and as long as I remember she always treated her plants and garden like her babies. She always said plants need love to grow as much as they need water and sunshine. She actually had these loving conversations with her garden plants.

The truth is everything in this world is energy and energy is either positive or negative. According to what we learn in quantum physics, it seems life is more of an energy flow than what meets the eyes What that means for us is that if we are aware of our own emotions we can stay conscious of the energy we contain, and hence creating the realities we desire is only a matter of deliberate choice. Change your vibration and you can change your reality. Now I know it sounds somewhat absurd to some of you but it is true. If we're feeling down about something, we can choose to change the situation and raise our own energy levels. I believe every word we use can either raise or dampen our energy levels. So using power-packed words can help us obtain the kind of powerful life that we all deserve to live. With a renewed perspective and a higher, more positive energetic vibration, which every single word we utter would influence, we have a much better chance of bringing good into our lives, rather than bitterly repeating old mistakes. Once again I say it is about what's familiar to our mind. If we make positive highly charged words part of our life there is no reason for the mind not to deliver the very best for us.

Now I know some of you might find the concept of energy a little off your thinking radar. Many find it really difficult to absorb the concept of all and everything around us including ourselves being energy! But I want to simplify it here, let's say you don't want to agree on the energy and its immense effect on everyone and our lives, can we safely say that how we feel, our emotions, have a huge impact on what we do how we perceive our lives and even our relationships?

We can reach a place in life where every emotion can be in our control, where we can create the emotion we desire at the moment and that is not only possible it can be so empowering that you begin to feel like a superhero of your own life

Let me explain how you can achieve this:

Every emotion has a trigger. If you can control this trigger you can choose your emotion. Now you must ask me how?

It is as simple as I say it. The biggest single trigger for our emotions is our thoughts !!!!

Yes, control the thoughts and you have your emotions under control. Our thoughts are initiated with the words we use for ourselves and from the circumstances we are in and there it is we have gone a full circle and we are back to our Self-talk.

Let's see an example:

Self-talk: I am so stupid .just can't make up my mind ....blah blah

Thoughts: I have to make a choice and if I don't it will ruin everything. Don't know what to do. Nothing will work right. I will not make the right choice blah blah...

Emotion: Anxiety, worry, distress, sadness,

Energy: Negative for sure which will very obviously attract more negativity

This is what I like to call The WTF loop (Word Thought Feeling Loop). which can be a vicious circle of continuous existence in our daily life until we completely understand the importance of our self-talk.

I would love to quote Dr Shad Helmster from his brilliant book "What to say when you talk to yourself" This book simply changed my life many years ago and I could never look back.

I am eternally grateful for all that I learnt. I especially love one of his analogies. He calls our subconscious mind a mental apartment that is filled with old broken and hands down furniture. This furniture has been handed down from parents, teachers, peers, society (the furniture he talks about are our thoughts and beliefs) He goes on to describe if we empty and throw out all this furniture and end up with an empty apartment, as delightful as it might seem to begin with but the mind which always goes back to what's familiar, will only take a short while before it goes back to drag every broken old piece of furniture back into the apartment why? Because our mind is not used to the empty clean place. So He, of course, suggests we need to replace the furniture immediately with new, beautiful ones which is your positive power-packed self-talk.

Understanding the connection between our words, thoughts and emotions is the gateway to controlling our own emotions. For so many of us when asked why we are feeling sad, the answer is "I don't know" and this is simply because we are unaware of the chain of thoughts that triggered the emotion. Even worse we are so on default mode that we don't realize the words that started the vicious circle WTF.

You see no matter how we analyze the way we feel we go back to our WORDS.

Whilst I am a total advocate of finding ways to have a choice on what emotions we experience and how we feel I also completely acknowledge the fact that feelings cannot and shouldn't be ignored or suppressed.

Most mental illnesses arise from suppressed emotions which in time can even manifest into physical dis-ease. The uneasiness that is created within our being due to the suppressed and bottled up emotions can create cysts, fibroids, even cancer. I have known so many who suffer from cancer and almost all of them after going through therapy have accepted that there is an area of their life that has been bothering them and the resentment that has been a baggage of negative energy and such a burden in their lives.

Unfortunately, not everyone is ready to acknowledge and accept the root cause of their resentment. Many would rather give up on life than understand the depths of their own emotions.

Once again, it is living mindfully that can help us face our deepest fears, guilt, anger and resentments. Once we learn to recognize these signs quickly it becomes such a natural process that we wouldn't allow the emotions to ever suffocate our energy channels. This is much easier than you imagine.

In this book, my efforts are to bring our attention to the truth that as we all desire to be parents someday or we are already parents, it only makes sense for us to clear the dust and garbage out of our own minds. We need to understand how our mind works, how our subconscious recordings are making us say things or do stuff which probably we are not very proud of.

But yet, we do end up saying things that don't seem to make even ourselves feel great never mind the child who looks up to us, literally.

I like to share some practical tips to stay in awareness of our words and thoughts, our WTF Loop. If consciously and repeatedly followed

The simplest way to do this is by these steps

Monitor: Monitor how you talk to yourself. Be aware of the number of negative words and sentences you use every day. Live in awareness and you will be surprised how many critical and negative comments you use for yourself and the life situations you face every day. Monitoring your words can be the first and most important step towards mastering your mind and getting hold of your emotions and your energies.

Edit: Once you are living mindfully, in awareness of your words it is crucial to edit these words and sentences into positive, constructive ones instantly. When you hear yourself saying " I am stupid" you got to change it immediately " I always know what's right for me" or whatever positive statement works for you. The idea of instant editing is to rewire what we have been used to for years and years. This process cannot be achieved so quickly, but the important point is to start as quickly as possible. Imagine, it has taken us years to reach the programming that we are at, the one that self-criticizes, so for sure we need to invest some conscious effort in editing these programs to ones that are self-appreciating and encouraging, through our self-talk.

Repetition: The key ingredient to reprogramming the subconscious mind and recreating what will be empowering and filled with positive energy is **repetition.** Our mind has been hearing the same self-demeaning talk for so many years and that is the reason we take and accept all that as the **Truth.** For so many of us, these statements were what we heard repeatedly from significant people in our lives while growing up and the repetition only made us believe them to be true. In some ways, they were written in stone just because they were repeated. That's the power of repetition.

These steps can help you to work out a process to achieve a level of mindfulness that can, not only help to control thoughts and emotions also maintain the energy levels in our consciousness.

CHAPTER 6

GIVE YOUR CHILD THE GIFT

When I talk about how parents must be mindful of the choice of words while in conversation with their children, I usually get a mixed reaction. Some show keen interest while many dismiss the idea. I believe they find the idea too constraining and binding.

Like every other parent, I too am convinced that once we become parents, we have an obligation to our children to give them the best future. The only difference in my thought process is that in order to guarantee their bright future, the best weapon we can hand them is a high level of self-esteem.

We, parents, have the power to help our children see themselves as heroes or Zeroes!!!

And once again, at the expense of boring you dear readers, it all goes back to the words we use with our young ones.

Some people believe in pragmatic parenting. "Don't raise a child's hope to be someone he can't be"

I have a question for all of you here and Who decides what the child can or can't be ???

Have we not read stories of great successes by the most unlikely personalities?

Albert Einstein was a school dropout.

Edison's teacher told his mother that he was useless and it was best she wouldn't invest in his education.

Hellen Keller was deaf and blind by the age of one and a half yet she went on to take the Braille language to another level. She mastered many languages even though she was not only blind also deaf. She went on to be the first deaf and dumb graduate from a well-known university.

It is so easy to let the negative critical voice that we all are so familiar with take over us and we transfer the same to our children.

Yes, maybe you didn't have a parent who encouraged you to be whoever you want to be.

Maybe your parents didn't know any better because their parents hadn't taught them that they can create their lives as they desire.

 Maybe you feel you got the raw end of the bargain in life,

Maybe you live with regret every single day of your life

Maybe you still sigh aloud when you remember that one wish as a child which you had to let go of because they made you believe life is not easy.

Maybe so many things ...

But today as parents we can change all that for our children. They don't have to live to be cynical, negative, bitter adults who never dare to dream because someone told them "You can't have it all"

We become who we think we are:

"A man is literally what he thinks, his character being the complete sum of all his thoughts."

— James Allen, As a Man Thinketh

The thoughts, of course, arise in a child's mind triggered by the words he hears from the most important people in his first 5 years of life.

As Aristotle said: "Give me a child for 7 years and I will give you the man" these are the years that will make a child into an adult who believes he can conquer the moon or one who hides away in fear of failure, rejection and disapproval.

We all desire approval. We all have the need to feel great. Unfortunately, as children, we are looking at our parents constantly for these words of approval which we will hold onto with all our might to create an image. That image is how we see ourselves, through the eyes of our mother or father, the eyes of our favourite teacher or aunt and uncle.

The need for approval makes the child accept whatever it is that the parent says. The urge to survive and be loved along with the need for approval from the significant people in the child's life literally takes away the innate KNOWING that we are all born with. The one and only thing the child knows is, to agree with the big persons is the way to their hearts and sure way to make them love me.

For a child who has been born with infinite self-love and self-confidence, it is such an irony that within a few years of living on this amazing planet amongst the people, the adults, who unfortunately mostly have got it all backwards when comes to their very own self-worth and self-image, he or she loses all that confidence. This is how children turn into these helpless little beings at the mercy of every word that adults utter.

Have you ever seen the little boy or girl who is trying to learn to ride a bicycle? The expecting eyes fixated on the father who is holding the seat, awaiting a word of encouragement: You can do this!"

That's all the kid wants to know," does my father believe in me?"

I never got to learn to ride a bicycle and believe it or not I still don't know why didn't my parents bother to think every child wants to learn to ride a bike, or rather has to learn to ride a bike!!!

Probably they were too busy or too thoughtless!!!!

It doesn't matter now. Not anymore, but for many years of my life I never ever asked for anything and do you want to know why this was the case?

It simply was that as a child I had asked and I was refused without an explanation or not heard is probably more apt. Now I know once again so many will be thinking " this is a blame game." Not at all, this was my process of looking for answers to the way my life was turning out.

In fact, there is no blame, because I know for sure they didn't know any better, They didn't think it would matter. But to me, it DID. It took many many sessions of hypnotherapy to understand the reason behind my lack of willingness to ask for anything. "The fear of rejection", and it all stemmed from many years ago when a 5 years old wanted to learn to ride a bicycle.

I am beginning to wonder if some of you might take this book as my very own personal rant about my childhood, at the cost of it looking that way I intend to self-disclose in order to bring my reality into the limelight. Every one of us has these shadows that we have to live with. Only many of us don't ever get around acknowledging the skeleton in the closet.

I did, I do and I am so glad that I did it.

Cleansing the TRASH, what I would like to call all those limiting beliefs and programs which were planted within our subconscious mind, is the only way to reach a place of peace, and total Realization. You ask what? Let's move on....

Today while I was pondering on the next series of my podcast, I had a thought about self-growth.

Like a seed that has to go through all the pain of growing its roots through the mud and stones inward towards the centre of the earth, and only then, can it begin to grow its beautiful green leaves. We need to dig into our very own depth. Yes, we will have to allow the roots to go through the dirt and it is not always pleasant. But once the roots are strong, that is when the real glory begins. "The sapling and soon the blossoms". And that is what we need. We all need strong roots. Once there are fruits on the plant of our personality, that is the time others can benefit so much from our growth.

Now some of us like truly yours, had to go through decades of life before ever getting her roots strong enough to begin the journey to bloom. It took years and years of harsh self-discovery to blossom and spread the fragrance of my inner wisdom

But some of us are, luckier, and those can be our children. That's because we know better, as parents.

I take full pride in my relationship with my kids. I can see confidence and self-love in them and that for me is my job well done.

It is so easy for a child to develop self-loathe and for nothing. Just because his or her parents never told her how great he is. Never told her that she is worth it. That she can speak her mind. That no question is a stupid one and that we can always learn what we don't know.

As I started this chapter, I like to finish it with a truth.

Just because you tell your child she can be whoever she wants, just because you tell your child that she is enough exactly as she is, just because she knows she can ask for whatever she wants.

(Asking does not equate to getting) The ability to ask on its own is an extremely powerful tool that most of us grow up, without.

"ASKETH AND YOU SHALL RECEIEVETH " a quote from the bible.

It says it all. All we need to learn and teach our children is simply to know that they can ask. While asking doesn't guarantee getting, but the attitude opens doors to possibilities and as mentioned in the bible, you will get what you deservedly asked for.

Just because of all that:

"She will not turn into a Narcissist. She will NOT be a spoilt child."

What you are giving her is the gift of Self-Value.

What you are giving her is the gift of "I AM ENOUGH"

And yes sometimes or probably mostly it is going to be hard work to get what she wants but at least she will never give up without giving it her all and that's what matters.

She will never start anything with a lack of self-belief.

She will never doubt her worthiness to thrive for what she desires for herself.

That is the kind of being who Knows Herself in the true sense of the word.

CHAPTER 7

"USE POWERFUL WORDS TO HAVE A POWERFUL LIFE"

This is one of my most favourite quotes. I think it needs to be written all over. We have to constantly be reminded of this.

This is exactly where the difference between the successful people of the world and the miserable, unhappy, dissatisfied ones will be seen with stark naked eyes.

Do you ever think a Ratan Tata or a Steve Jobs (bless his soul) or an inventor or Richard Branson or Morgan Freeman would say to themselves. " I suck at that I can't do this ???!

Their dictionary usually has no negative words in it especially the ones that would imply their own lack of ability, fortune, resources etc. I also acknowledge that we all including the successful personalities have our moments of low. But those who live in awareness of these moments and make quick corrections are the ones who reach the peak.

Perseverance in life is a product of self-belief. If you believe you can, you will NOT give up so easily on something that you desire to learn, have or acquire.

Self-belief is a direct product of how we see ourselves and that for most of us is dependent on how we see ourselves through the eyes of our significant people.

Now, I agree there have been very successful people who have grown up in less than lucrative or positive environments and yet they never let go of their beliefs. Yes, that is possible.

To me, that is where we all should reach and stay there. A place of self-reliance, total self-belief where nothing anyone else says matters because I have this cent per cent belief that "I can do this, I got this "

As we are concerned parents or to be parents who want to give a head start to our little ones.   This is our chance to make amends and learn exactly what and how can we steer our own lives so that we can guide the next generation into a bright future.

We don't want them to have to struggle to get where we are working so hard to get to. A place of confidence, that we know we have to want it bad enough and we can work towards it to achieve it.

We are here to see how we can say the right words when we talk to our little boy or girl so that they don't grow up wondering.

I have decided to make it as simple as possible for all of you out there. All of you, who have stuck by me, and have read this book this far. I am eternally grateful for your support and if you go ahead and apply all that we learnt together in this little book of my passion, I reassure you we will have a more " powerful life ".

So here I go and that is a list of most commonly used sentences and words which seem so innocent and yet so harmful for a child, and of course the edited version of it.

Yes, as parents there are so many times that we have to correct our kids. We have a moral obligation to teach them the good and bad, what's right and what's wrong.

It is never the intention that is under the question, it is only the HOW and WHAT that must be kept in check.

Our words can be twisted to our advantage, they can be replaced with ones that are power-packed and only send a message of "YOU ARE ENOUGH" to our child.

It is interesting to notice if as a parent, you practice this, you will find the magic happening in your own life as well. If we are consciously being positive for the purpose of sending the right message to our child imagine the effect that we will have on our own minds!

As they say " kill two birds with one stone" opppsss not a nice Idiom since I am a Vegan. Probably, "Feeding two birds with a scone makes better sense."

Ps. Awareness of choice of words can both empower and help you learn new vocabulary.

I hope you are looking forward to upgrading your set of frequently used phrases ☺

What NOT to say	What we NEED to say
NO, because I said NO	I believe it is not possible, we can discuss
Don't do that (for every small act)	You can try carefully
You are going to drop	Focus on what you are holding
You are going to break that	Keep your eyes on what you are carrying
You can't complete that.(painting/project etc)	If you work hard you probably will nearly complete it
If you don't study how will you pass	You realize in order to achieve good grades you have to put some work in
What have you forgotten again?	What did you remember now?
You are very messy	I know it is not fun to keep cleaning but to find them next time you have to put them back

You are not good at	I am certain if you give it your best and practice you can get very good at...
You eat what's on your plate!	I agree probably this is too much for you, but this time if you finish it. next time we will see to it that you are served less
You eat whatever has been cooked for you even if you don't like it	I will listen to the reason you don't like this meal but you have to listen to momma and the reasons I want you to eat this.
Please don't do drama, it is not that bad and it is good for your health	Why do you think this food is disgusting? Can you eat some because it will make you stronger? And perhaps I can serve something you like tomorrow!
Don't speak when not spoken to!	It is good manners to wait for your turn to speak, that way everyone can listen to what you have to say
Don't interrupt me when I am talking to you!	I need you to listen to me carefully first and then I promise to listen to whatever you have to say(KEEP YOUR PROMISE)
You can't be an actor, artist, singer,...richest man	I believe you can be whatever you wish to be if you put your mind to it and take action but believe me I am sure you will

	change your mind a few times by the time you grow up
You are not good with your hands, languages, math....	I know it might seem difficult right now but there is nothing you cannot learn if you have the will and if you practice enough
You can't have that... toy...	I believe if you want it you need to earn it so what are you going to do in that case?
I can't afford that...	Well, that is an expensive item that requires momma to save some money to get it. Do you think you can come up with ideas to save for it?
Do you think money grows on tree!	It is important to value the money that we work to bring home

What you see here is some of the most common conversations we all have with our kids around habits, food, toys, money, daily activities etc..

The list can be endless believe me. What I hope is to show the idea of how we can change our words to make the damage minimum. In fact to make every word so empowering that our child's take away from the conversation is one lesson closer to trusting that He/ She is ok, that He/ She can ask and not be dismissed by adults...

The feeling of "I am significant" is what we all need to feel. This is only possible when our thoughts, wishes and desires -no matter how silly - have been heard by the people we look up to.

In all my years of working with children of all ages, I noticed one common factor and that They all without an exception whether they say it aloud or not want you to listen to what they have to say. As a teacher, I was loved most because I listened. I am sure every teacher who is reading this would be in agreement with me. Favourite teachers are the ones who genuinely listen.

Every child has this overactive imagination with tons of thoughts and ideas running through it and all he or she wants is for someone to listen and listen with interest. And tell her /him that he is amazing for thinking all that.

What we adults forget along the way is that there was a time we were in that place. That we wanted to talk all day and needed our parents to listen. Somewhere, along the way, as our mother said "ok, go away now, I have to finish cooking" or our father was heard telling our mother " keep the kids quiet when I come home, I am tired" we decided to remain invisible and not express because what "they" do is much more important than what I have to say.

When the child wants his father to go out and play ball with him and all he hears, again and again, is "why don't you run along, I am too tired" He knows then, that he is not an important person.

Yes, I know at times life can get really tough on us as parents and that we are genuinely too washed out from the day's work and stress to be able to take another step.

What we have to remind ourselves is this:

It was I who decided to have a child.

It was I who should have planned my work and finances better before committing to be a parent.

It is I who wants to have more and probably give more to the child.(whom, mind you, will be happier with less material and more time spent playing or yapping with you)

You see, we have to take full responsibility for all our thoughts and actions and emotions.

Our children are here because we chose to bring them into this world and while it doesn't make them our private property that we can speak to, in any way we want or treat as we desire, They do NOT have to pay for our lack of competence, planning, energy or whatever excuse it is we come up with.

CHAPTER 8

IF ONLY OUR PARENTS KNEW

I know I have been really going harsh on parents here. Please don't take it personally "I am a Parent" and every word you read here is totally and completely directed at me. In fact, I have already analyzed, scrutinized and condemned myself after which I have accepted where I could have been a better mom. And Voila! Writing all about it here..

Now, I know how much of a pressure it is to be a parent, (at the cost of discriminating I have to say this), especially "to be a mother". Our society, families, culture, norms, and moral values create this immense and almost impossible to satisfy standards for Motherhood.

If we care too much, we are frowned upon.

If we are homemakers, we are not contributing.

If we are going to work, we neglect our kids.

If we feed too much, nana

If we feed too healthy, too fussy.

If we correct too much, we are controlling.

If we don't correct, we are spoiling.

And the list can go on and on.

I have been there and I feel the pressure for all of you. That's why I decided it was time for me to put a chapter in where I actually sympathize with your parents, with adults.

I know I have been more of an advocate for the young ones until now and that doesn't really change because the essence of my work is to create awareness amongst us, adults, as to the extent of influence we have on our children.

Yet I see it fair to talk about how difficult it is to be an adult, to be a parent.

All that you have read so far and hopefully you have learned this far, tell us what our parents had no clue about. They didn't know, how every word they say addressing us will manipulate how we see ourselves.

They didn't know because the information wasn't freely available. The research was in progress. They didn't know because they had grown up to believe what was, was right. The attitude of questioning "what is", refers more to the recent generation and the ones who have questioned life.

Why do I feel the way I do about myself?

Why is it that no matter how hard I try, there is a nagging voice that holds me back from going and getting what I desire?

Even though I know I am good at so many things, why is there an invisible power holding me back?

We questioned so we have answers today. We know the way our subconscious has been programmed by our parents, teachers and friends and family. We know while we were kids we had no control over these messages getting recorded in our subconscious mind.

But today, as grown-ups, we do not have to be at the mercy of those old and demeaning programs. We don't have to succumb to what is. We know we have the power to change these limiting programs and not only that we have the power to do so much more for our own children.

That is the essence of this book. My dear readers, this knowledge can be revolutionary for each one of us.

Don't we all desire to be great parents? I know I did, I still do.

Don't we all desire to see our children succeed? Soar high in the Sky of achievement? I know I do.

Don't we all want to see our children abundant with health, wealth, great relationships?

We all do, and we try every minute of our life to do the best for them but we go wrong when we forget that, they are empowered, highly able beings born to reach the stars and what we do by being ignorant to our power of words, is nothing short of destroying their natural, God-given self-confidence!!!! That sounds recipe for disaster for our offspring.

You see, I believe until we don't know any better it is all forgiven. If you don't know how powerful your words are, then it is all forgiven. That was the case with our parents, with my mother and yours, and yours ...... so many of us today look back and we KNOW exactly how those words we heard every day hurt us. Today we know better.

And that's why, as parents, as adults, we cannot be forgiven. After knowing, if you still want to have those negative self-talk or negative, abusive conversations with your child,

 THIS is NOT forgivable.

I, personally found this knowledge so empowering. The fact that I can, all on my own, change the programming in my mind (subconscious) made me feel like a creator.

This simply meant that I was not some helpless thing who had no choice in life.

Coming up with excuses for something that even though wasn't my choice, to begin with, but later by holding on to those thoughts I chose to give away my own power. Whining about things such as:

What should I do, my parents were.....

This is how I have been brought up...

My childhood was ....

Yes, we all have experiences that make us form a set of beliefs about life, relationships, how we look at ourselves. Even how we view the world around us and how we choose to react to the events. Unfortunately, majority of these beliefs do not belong to us.

 So we go on to blame someone or some event that got us to the point at which we find ourselves today. That, to me, doesn't seem very empowering!

Today I have turned the whole table around. How? I know exactly how to talk to myself. And in the process of the acknowledgement of the "power of my words" I KNOW exactly how to talk to my kids. Having claimed that, it doesn't imply that I am perfect or that I never mess up with regard to my kids. However, I like to reiterate, I AM AWARE OF MY WORDS TO EDIT THEM QUICKLY.

You see, words are the one thing that once out of your mouth, you simply cannot take them back, much as you might desire to do so.

In history, the pen has been compared to the sword because of the power the words possess.

As poetic as it sounds we do know that the power lies with the person who thinks the words and utters those to use as weapons to make or break the listener.

Words can either build you up or tear you down

The question is what do you choose for yourself

I have already shared some practical tools to check the WTF vicious circle that we all can get so terribly stuck with. Once you practice the art of controlling your mind,(words, thoughts, feelings) you will naturally change your diction. You will observe the use of negative words reducing to their minimum needed level.

Another tool that I am eternally grateful for is self-talk. As I have mentioned before once you are aware of your negative self-talk and you begin to edit your vocabulary, it is most crucial to replace these words in our dictionary with the right positive, encouraging words. The words that ignite an emotion of ecstasy and flight. Now some of you will laugh at the way I put it here but

Let's experiment.

BE honest, say each of these words aloud and check for the emotions that they evoke within you

Ecstatic,

Exemplary

Fantastic,

Fantabulous

Amazing

Exciting

Invigorating

Rejuvenating

Energizing

The list can go on but how many of these are part of your daily vocabulary?!!!

Please use powerful adjectives for yourself.

"I have an exemplary memory, I remember everything I read "

Instead of

"I have a terrible memory, can't remember anything"

"My body is fabulous, it digests whatever I eat "

Instead of

"I become fat no matter what I eat"

The above are the most common criticism I hear from clients. And believe it or not, I was right there a decade ago. Did that attitude serve me? A loud "NO".

Do I feel great today after the realization? Hell, YES.

I have to be crazy to go back to that self-talk after all that I have achieved. And the same goes with every one of you.

Did you actually feel the difference in the emotions that arise within you as you say the words in the list, aloud? I bet if you are honest you cannot deny it.

You see, we are always awaiting some praise, a few good words from others around us. The truth is that all that others say to us, no matter how much they praise or appreciate us doesn't have a dime of value in our minds. Why? That is because our mind is very smart and recognizes all those as some kind of a scam with an ulterior motive. Pretty cool, right?

I am sure you are thinking "but I enjoy the praises and the applauds, I want them, I need them"

The one that benefits from the compliments and outside praises is your Ego. But your mind, specifically your subconscious cares a hoot for what comes from outside of you.

So learn to say the right things to yourself. Praise, compliment, appreciate yourself and you will see the magic begin.

Now, this is not a quick fix as much as we would have loved it to be. You see it has taken us many years to get habituated to the set of vocabulary we use for ourselves or in general, so you cannot expect miracles to happen overnight. You have to consciously be at it until the entire old and broken furniture is out and our apartment (subconscious mind) has been refurbished with beautiful, useful and positive ones. This is a process and as you get to start it, I assure you, you will enjoy every bit of the change.

You feel better about yourself and life seems to get easier. The great poet Saadi from Persia writes in his Gulestan-e-saadi

"Life is as hard or as easy as you make it"

"Patience, everything seems hard before it becomes easy"

What wisdom! The very few who just knew even before science proved it all.

So let's take charge, let's create the life we desire by practising to write it our way.

Let's take life easy so that it will be easy

CHAPTER 9
QUESTIONS SUCCESSFUL PARENTS ASK THEMSELVES

Taking a rain check as a parent is one of the most important steps for a successful parent.

Whilst we have the best of our child at heart, it is crucial to ask some questions of ourselves and of course, response to those have to be with total honesty.

I have gathered some pointers for the questions which any parent who wants to be better than their own parents must ask themselves.

Do I want what seems safe & easy for my child or do I want what's best?

Now I know this sounds strange but the truth is many times we allow or guide our kids towards decisions that seem safe, achievable and probably even easy just because we love our kids and we want them to succeed. But the truth of the matter is that most great things in life require us to work with focus , total commitment and perseverance. It probably would entail taking a few risks and even a few falls. But the final result can be the best that happens to us.

This is what we need to want for our children. But....

Encouraging your children to go ahead and take a chance for what they desire to achieve is what a successful parent would do.

Do I finish every discussion with how much I love my child?

You see, as parents, we feel almost obliged to admonish our kids at times. This is what good parents do, right? However, no matter how the conversation ends or where it leads, it is most important to make sure your child knows that the discussion was only about the behaviour, and had nothing to do with you, loving your child. Make sure your child knows "Love does NOT change if he or she does not behave as you expected"

Do I measure my parental competence with the level of my control over my child's life?

I have seen so many parents who believe the one and the only way to be crowned a great parent is when you have full control over the child. This can only end up in bringing up a child who is deeply under-confident with very misconceived self-image. If you don't show your faith in your child's ability to make small decisions, or even at times big ones, there is no way your child would ever have any self-belief or self-trust.

Am I making my child live my desires?

When my daughter was barely 8 years old I observed her undeniable talent in beautifying everything around her. She had this impeccable eye for aesthetics (even today she can turn the ugliest thing into a piece of art) .So I was ecstatic to acknowledge, my daughter could accomplish, what I never could achieve in life which was go to a design school,. For the next few years, I encouraged her to take various training and it was years later that one fine day I had to face the reality. Yes, she is the most talented girl I have known however, her passion didn't completely lie in the design aspect. She has a love for business, branding and reaching the market along with a love and knowledge for luxury. I realized I was forcing her to do what I couldn't, all those many moons ago.

To be a successful parent, we have got to check whether we are pushing our kid to do what we regret every minute of our life for not having done!!!!

Do I set my child for success?

Now, I know this has been repeated a million times so far but the whole point of this book is for us adults, parents or parents to be, to live in awareness of the power of our own words.

Are you telling your child again and again that he or she can succeed in any task that he sets his mind on? The words that come from a parent are the pillars of a successful future for your child. It is almost ridiculous how seriously we take our parents' words, but truth be told we all do. After all, our parents who give us life, bring us into this world, aren't they next to "The Almighty" for us? And we are or soon going to be the God for another being, our son or daughter.

Yes, the burden can be very difficult to bear but this is what it is. Parents can make or break their child !!!!

Am I using such sentences often enough? such as

"I am proud of you"

" No matter what, I will always love you"

"I am surprised at your behavior but that does not mean my love for you changes"

"Thank you "

"I am here for you "

"What do you want?"

"What do you think on .... matter ?"

"I am sorry."

"Can you forgive me?"

"I made a mistake."

"I shouldn't have lost my temper"

So many of us assume that our kids know how much we love them, or how proud we are of them. We take it for granted that there is no need for articulation. Alas, as your actions can speak louder than words, yet to hear such reassuring, supportive words from a parent can build up a solid indestructible foundation. Say it aloud!

Do I feel responsible "for" my child or "towards" my child?

There is a difference here. Let me explain. It is absolutely essential for a parent to be responsible towards the child you bring into this world, safety, basic needs, love and affection, education and medical care. Yes of course, what we need to learn as parents is that we are not responsible for them. You ask what does that mean? It means the child's life and actions and decisions that he or she will make are very much his or her own responsibility. Most of us feel responsible for our children to the extent of feeling guilty when things don't seem right "to us" and of course gloat with pride when they do go in the direction we assume is worthy of pride. If you nurture the thought of "being responsible for your child's emotions and actions", the only thing you achieve is a sense of control. This in turn can be a major factor in damaging your relationship with your child. Remember No one likes to be controlled.

Let go with respect while you are still responsible towards your child.

The bottom line is we all, each and every one of us, is responsible for our own lives. Our actions, emotions and decisions are ours and the pain or pleasure too.

Once you get this as a parent you will find it much easier to have a decent, amicable and successful relationship with your childern especially as they enter into their adulthood.

Do I teach my child that what she does defines her or who she is?

I have to use this quote here because it says it all

> *Many succeed momentarily by what they know;*
>
> *Some succeed temporarily by what they do;*
>
> *Few succeed permanently by what they are.*
>
> *(Anonymous)*

What we have to ask ourselves is do we want to set our kids for permanent success, or not!

Do I encourage my child to make commitments towards things and tasks or do I emotional blackmail /force him or her into it?

So many parents, in the name of "I have the best at heart for you" literally force their child into classes, activities, courses, careers, friendships, even marriages that the child never wanted to commit to!!

And what do you think would happen in such a scenario? Do you think your child is set for success if he has been pushed to make a choice he hates? Yes many of us have been there, jobs we hate and relationships we regret forever. All that, just to please a parent.

A successful parent must know that the only way you can get your child to commit to something is by showing him what he can get at the end of the road. Convince her/him, not emotionally blackmail. Talk it out, discuss the pros and cons of committing or not. If your child has made a decision based on facts, the likelihood of sticking by the decision is many folds more than you trying to force her/him into it.

Remember You are not responsible for your child.

If things go great the crown is hers and if they don't, She will have to learn to face whatever it is. All you can promise is that you will be there and you will love her no matter what the outcome.

Do I set the right example for my child to be a positive, receiving individual?

Most of us are constantly cribbing about our days, our jobs. How we had a bad day at the office or even worse we are trash-talking behind someone we probably spend a lot of time with. That could be in-laws or even so-called friends.

You see, if I cannot be carrying a positive and calm disposition at least most of the time, there is no way my child is going to be what he or she doesn't see in front of her.

As we have discussed before, your children see you through the strongest lens you can imagine. They observe and analyze and absorb all your told and untold messages. The energy that you emit is what your child can sense better than any other person. Children and animals are the best judges of character. That's why if you want to know about a person, you can ask your child.

They say " Hear the truth from a child"

The only problem is that most of the time we are not ready to hear that truth especially if it points at ourselves.

So, make sure you practice what you preach. Your child has the right to ask you "How can I be calm when you are screaming on top of your voice at me?" or "why should I feel great about my school, when you seem to constantly complain about your work?"

Again I know some of you might wonder, it is not for a child to ask such questions because kids are not supposed to talk this way to their parents!!!! If you are one who is thinking this

MY REQUEST GO BACK AND RESTART THE BOOK FROM BEGINNING

CHAPTER 10

A PARENT'S JOB

I have tried to find ways to reach out to parents or those going to be. While I am super passionate about the mere power of our words and even more so of the subconscious programming which we assumed, is not in our control – now we know better – I also am not oblivious to the tough or rather toughest job that it is to be a parent.

At times it feels, we just can never get it right. I have called being a parent " a thankless job" and to a great extent I still do believe it to be that.

No matter how hard we try to better ourselves, resolve our own childhood issues, work on our forgiveness and acceptance. Live more mindfully and learn how to be more friends to our children than authoritative parents, we still have days we hear our 7 years old screaming "You are a bad momma, I hate you" or our 13 years old shutting the bedroom door on our face while we are still talking, or even worse our 16 years old disappointedly saying "You don't get me, you never get me" And God! does that hurt?

You see the truth is, I would love to say "my kids never lie to me", I also want to say "they are super healthy mentally", or they think "I am the greatest mom on earth" … unfortunately that is not the case.

We do our best. I always repeat to all my clients, that there is no notion such as perfection and as parents, we cannot be perfect. Because as we discovered earlier we, too, had parents who f*** us up, of course, unknowingly. And unless we all decide to go through therapy before becoming parents, we definitely will have our unique set of challenges in bringing mentally sound children into the future. I also understand the previous sentence might have shocked you, wondering if I am recommending therapy to everyone. Probably some of you might also question my authority to say this.

My own and so many other's experiences have been evidence to me that we all can benefit from some level of professional help. This is not to demean anyone and say something is wrong but definitely helps in sorting our own minds and life.

The more sorted we are, the better we can guide our children, and the healthier and closer our relationship with our children.

This chapter is all about a reality check. Having out of the world expectations of ourselves as adults will not help. Whilst we learnt a whole lot about how we can influence our kids and how it all begins with cleaning our own closet from the cobwebs of the past -our own childhood – no one said it will be a smooth ride.

Let's remember that.

I have come across parents who beat themselves up for every little thing that goes wrong with their children. We are not responsible for their choices and actions. What we are responsible for is to give them all the tools they require to be fully equipped to take the right actions, to make the right decisions. That's the end of our control.

You say, "I read it all and I have brought up my kids following every tip I see in here and yet today I seem to be at constant war with my teenage child, he/she doesn't want to do much in life, doesn't listen to me or talk to me blah blah...."

You see there is an unwritten rule amongst teenagers especially and that is "If I listen to my parents I am not grownup"

For every kid from the very beginning it is all about:

"I need to feel significant"

Even your two years old would insist on doing everything on his own "I can do it myself" is all you hear and that actually means "I am important, I am capable"

Later your teenager will be shouting repeatedly "chill, I got this ", and why do you think is that? Because:

"I need to feel significant"

I know it looks like we have come a full circle but it all comes to the same simple rules which we have been going through. Once we know the rules it makes it so much easier to understand and accept the behaviour of our children.

Having said all this, our commitment as parents is to create strong steady foundations. Do what you know, what you learnt. Believe that your every effort to build up your child with the magnificent power of your words will NOT go to waste. Even though, he is throwing tantrums apparently or not hearing you.

To be totally honest, if you start early and do it right, I don't see how you will ever be disappointed.

Gandhi said "Be the change you want to see in others"

So let's change ourselves as parents, we will definitely see it in our kids. And this is why I keep reiterating the importance of working out our own issues before committing to parenthood.

In a recent interaction with a mother of 4 year old, she asked me for tips on handling her little one because he has become very "stubborn" !!

The first thing that came into my mind was 'there we go a TAG"

Do you catch what I am cooking!! (a Scottish saying for Do you get what I say) ☺

What I had to explain to the mother was the very basic rule. I am beginning to sound like a broken tape but the little boy needs to know he is important. He wants to prove to his mother that he can do everything on his own, and that he still has the confidence to ask for whatever he wants. He wants to have her APPROVAL. Bingo! This is exactly the junction that the mother has got to know how important her words will be to that child's subconscious recording. He NEEDS the mother to affirm that He is OK.

She can scream, punish, shout, TAG or

She can communicate with empowering words and speak of CHOICE. I explained to the mother that as human beings we have the power to choose but we need to have choices for that. Every child, too, deserves to be given options to choose from. I know for some parents, this, again, sounds like too much work. Some might even say "I never was given any choices by my parents." But imagine if you had been given, how different would have your beliefs towards "freedom to choose" been! This is a clear example of limiting beliefs that were fed into our programming system without our conscious awareness.

As grownups, we have choices. Right? What to eat, when to sleep, what to wear, when and what to speak. These are our basic choices, right? But we refuse to offer even these to our children! In the name of, "I know what's best for you" Or worse, some parents think they NEED to control every move of their child just because they are Parents.

Let's play more...

As adults, some of us have had the freedom to choose our bigger decisions in life, like our life partner or our profession or the car, and the house we bought. How did that feel? How would that feel if you didn't have those choices?

Some others were not that lucky. They had to follow the stick. I bet that wasn't a pleasant experience. Not having a say in the profession you choose! Or the life partner you have to live with for the next 50, 60 years!

And yet, so many of us don't see why a child needs freedom of choice! It is the case with so many of us. Why?

Because somewhere, in the circle of parent-child-parent, the belief was passed on that "Kids don't know what's good for them", the value of "freedom of choice" was overlooked. This limiting belief was passed on from subconscious to subconscious generation after generation. How many suffered a life of dissatisfaction and misery and despair along the way???!!

Back to the 4 year- old boy who is called "stubborn". I would say after reading all that you did in this book, by now I hope that you can guess who needs to change or relearn what was wrongly taught to them?

If as parents or adults who will be future parents someday, we get these concepts. If we start to clear the skeletons in our own closet. If we recognize the limiting beliefs, acknowledge them, accept them and let those go. We won't have to worry about how we handle our kids now or later. Because we know better.

I acknowledge that there is no foolproof remedy or guarantee for attaining perfection. That is because perfection is just a concept. What is perfect in one's perspective need not necessarily be seen as perfect by others.

However, knowing how our subconscious mind works and the importance of our words in creating the life that we truly desire, is a life-changing transition that is worth all the efforts.

"You are only as limited as your beliefs."

— *Jennifer Ho-Dougatz*

Chapter 11

AND FINALLY

Psychology has been a field that was avoided by most people for years. Whether it is an educated person or a simple layman soul. Not many really were willing to get into the complex web of our conscious mind, leave alone the subconscious.

Today this science of understanding the mind has gone beyond and above all that was expected. You must be thinking "am I here to read about your psychological jargon?" No, I agree you are here to understand yourself better in order to make sure you are the best influence possible for your kids.

But whilst I was in contemplation of going to the final chapter, I had this urge to remind everyone who is reading this book of the truth about human beings. That's US

You see a couple of decades ago, a branch of psychology called "positive psychology" was introduced to the world by Martin Seligman.

Without getting into details that might only interest a psychology student I want us to understand another proven fact.

We are inherently created to KNOW that which is good for us. We are not broken people, or helpless. We are not about our miseries and disorders. You see for many years psychology only meant working with someone who is suffering from a disorder and needs professional help. Perhaps for the same reason, so many were afraid of ever admitting they needed to reach out to a psychologist because that meant that they suffered from a mental disorder.

Back to our innate ability, to reach for the happiness and satisfaction at the epicenter of our very own being. Yes, that is what we are, who we truly are.

We have the ability to minimize negative pathological thought patterns and take away the helplessness and lack of self-esteem that comes along with it.

We can change the negative self-image that I have been talking about, created by our destructive belief system which we almost always inherit and not self-create.

There have been numerous researches proving that focus on the positive, along with a series of mindfulness practices can improve levels of anxiety and depression.

Positive psychology is based on humanistic approach of Carl Rogers, Abraham Maslow and others who emphasized on the innate goodness of human beings. That we are not born to self sabotage and that people innately do not have bad intentions.

So keeping this in mind we must acknowledge our own power to do good not only to others, to ourselves too. And if we end up messing our own lives or the lives of our children somewhere along the way, it is not because we are born that way or we have this sadistic pleasure in self-destruction.

To put it in the simplest words we are lost. We have forgotten who we are and it is as simple as that.

When we are born all we need is life and love.

On the way out of this physical body, all we need is love.

It is somewhere in between that the exposure to so much input from our surroundings messes with who we truly are and we lose our way.

Mind you I am not implying that you should be living in a glass house so that you don't get affected by all the negative that can divert you from staying in touch with your Inner Being, your Highest self, your Consciousness.

That's why the most important purpose in everyone's life is to develop a loving relationship with oneself. To be in constant sync with the power within.

I sincerely recommend a meditation routine which in time will definitely lead to an all-time mindfulness state that keeps you in conscious awareness of your words, thoughts, emotions and actions.

Each time you sense a negative emotion it is a clear indication that you are out of synch. This is your notification and the reminder that you need to attend to some kind of negative or unhelpful aspect of your life.

You ask if it is that simple! I say it is not but it all begins with:

1. Understanding your own greatness
2. The willingness to live a full life with emotional wellbeing
3. The awareness that you want more from this life

We are all work in progress almost our entire lives and that is the beauty of us. We are all about motion. Moving forward whether it is physically or emotionally is who we are.

The best way to look at our personal growth and development is:

"Enjoy the journey and the destination would seem so much more achievable."

EPILOGUE

I have been talking so much about the mind and how we need to learn the rules of the mind to master control over our words, thoughts, and emotions. By now I am sure it all seems a lot clearer that what we think is a direct result of what words we use most frequently and that our thoughts lead to our emotions which in turn lead to how we react or respond to any situation in life.

Clarity on this simple yet difficult concept to follow can change our daily lives forever.

So I was in deep thoughts about the simple fact that we all need a purpose in life and this probably is the main pain point for so many of us. What is my purpose? We all ask a million times or at least most of you or you wouldn't be reading a book such as this one.

After years of seeking and wondering I have realized that our very purpose as human beings is to know ourselves and once we truly know who we are, to have unconditional self-love for that we truly are. Does that make sense to you?

Do you see why we need to be kinder and more compassionate towards ourselves in order to use the better, more positive and more encouraging words so that we can build the kind of self-confidence, self -love with which we were born? This is all because we have to get back to that original knowledge that "we are that universal energy or consciousness. We are the image of that creator or the inner being or the higher self. Whatever you want to call this energy and as I have implied before this energy is within every being. That is the commonality that binds all living beings in this universe together."

The simple truth is our purpose in this world is to learn self-love and why shouldn't we love ourselves unconditionally? We are so much more than the body or the features that we criticize so often. We are more than what we are made to believe. We are "The Truth " I like to call us that. "The Truth" to me is that which is all-knowing, capable of all creations and filled with so much universal love that can over-flow to everyone and everything surrounding it.

Such grandiosity, such pure love, such power can only be loved and adored.

This is not self-centeredness, this is not narcissism, this is awareness of our greatness and this awareness must only lead to self-adoration in its healthiest form. This in turn will lead us to create the life, the relationships, the job, the house, the abundance that we deserve.

"Everything is simplicity, there is nothing to do.

There is no place to go.

There is no thing to become.

You are that, just the way you are.

Awaken to your true Self which is what you are right now."

— *Robert Adams*

Ponder on these golden words and you will know there is really no chase in this world. There is nowhere to go to, life is surely not a race because each destination seems to be the starting point for the next race. But the question is where are we trying to reach and why are we in this constant chase for happiness or is it abundance or ....what?

We are indeed at the destination right from the start.

The problem is as soon as we open our eyes into this world, we forget that simple fact that "We are That" the highest energy, the inner being, the ultimate consciousness.

Unfortunately

All that we believe we are is the exact opposite of what we truly are .....

Take a moment to digest this.

You see all the limiting beliefs that we spoke about, which mostly are the unwanted gifts from our parents, and the environment makes us more limited every living moment.

Now you wonder how do we go back to the original ....how do we recognize the greatness of ourselves?

By working on the destructive, limiting beliefs that give rise to the way we speak, to ourselves as self-talk, or to others. These beliefs manifest into thoughts that only hold us back from "The Knowing" . While we are going from pillar to post to acquire this and that, all we need to really do is Know ourselves.

Knowing oneself is a concept that seems so alien to most. Today I understand the value of the question "who am I?" Once we truly understand the meaning of this the world as we know it will transform into a haven where we are the king or queen of it.

I know for many of you reading this, it all seems too heavy and probably even to a great extent unbelievable or even nonsensical. Some who are more open to a better life for themselves would ask HOW. How do we reach a place of total self-love and complete self-belief?

My answer to that is By Living in Awareness.

— Drew Gerald

Mindfulness practices can be life-changing if exercised on a regular basis.

Have you in actuality ever taken the time to

1. Listen to the sounds in your surrounding
2. Watch the birds that fly
3. Notice exactly the small details of the roads you have been frequenting perhaps for days, weeks or months
4. Have you listened to someone with full attention without planning what to say next in response?
5. Have you observed the trees along the park you take your walk
6. Have you observed if your inhales are belly full and exhales are belly flat

I know, all of these steps towards awareness can sound so simple and ridiculous at first glance, and yet I urge you to read them a few times and humor yourself with an honest answer to each.

If your response is mostly Yes, I am proud of you and so should you be. You are right on track. However, if there are few NOs there, how about giving these a sincere shot??

Once you decide to practice being mindful, you can ask yourself every now and then during the day "Am I in Awareness?"

As soon as you ask this question you will be amazed how your mind shuts down as if to make way for your awareness.

Whilst you practice mindful -living, you will be more mindful of your words, thoughts and emotions. You will be mindful and in sync with your higher self, the intuition that guides you to make the choices you make and all this can only lead to the creation of a Life you Desire.

As this awareness grows you will realize the difference between "YOU -The higher self" and "you- the body".

BINGO That's exactly where we want to get to.

Isn't this what we all have been chasing after?

"Manifestation of our ideal world"

None can happen unless we know who we are!!!!

"Your own Self-Realization is the greatest service you can render the world."

— Ramana Maharshi

As Maslow expressed in his hierarchy of needs, it is self-actualization that is our ultimate goal. All the rest seems mundane once we understand what is the real purpose here.

I also know as Maslow put it we need to acquire the basic needs first before we reach there. And yet I would say if the truth is understood with full clarity, having the life that we desire which is secure with clothing, food, shelter and the love of others can be manifested by choice.

We all have the need to trust something or someone. The one and the only person that needs to be trusted completely is YOURSELF.

Nothing can destroy our daily happiness more than a lack of trust and belief in ourselves. This is where it all begins. The doubts, the "I am not enoughs", the "I cannot do this", and LIFE SUCKS!

Life is beautiful when we know why we are here.

I love to know your response to a simple question

WHO ARE YOU?

I am always amused by the definitions we have for ourselves.

I am Shadi, a mother, wife, daughter, a therapist, a writer.... And so on

What we don't realize is that we are much more than this.

Compassionate, confident, amazing, honest, caring, funny, active, capable, so many other things that can define me as I am. Most of us do not see ourselves in the true sense and that is the main reason we are constantly awaiting someone to come along and tell us who we are!

You are such a nice person. You are handsome or pretty ...

If you could see yourself as you truly are you would have no NEED for another person's definition of you. The problem here is, not everyone would define you in the way you like to hear. You see, that is when our life turns around when others have definitions that tear us down, destroy our self-image and self-worth. It all begins when someone tells us we cannot be anything good when someone says we are useless, or not smart, or so many other undesirable tags.

Is it not better to know ourselves so that we live an emotionally independent life. Independent of the opinion of others of us.

Once we reach a place of total self-realization and complete self-love, we can be emotionally so independent that we don't live from a point of focus on the need to hear from others who we are or what we are good at.

I believe as parents we have a duty to make sure we create the environment and the playground for our children that leads them to emotional independence, true self-love and deep self-belief which they are born with.

There is nothing more liberating than being able to decipher our emotions and use them just as guiding beacons to self-understanding. The knowledge of self helps us to be in a state of joy and happiness. Isn't this what all of us want?

What we don't get is that Happiness is a state independent of all other emotions and events. I know you must be wondering how can I be in a state of happiness when something has upset me?

You can if you recognize that just because at this moment something has caused you pain, it does not have to be directly connected to your being happy or rather unhappy!!!

My genuine efforts in this book have been, to complete the circle of how we can feel empowered and be the creators that we truly were born to be. Knowing oneself and also acknowledging the immense responsibility we have towards the generations that come after us.

This journey is not easy but every bump and hurdle along the way carries its own precious lesson.

People say Life is not supposed to be easy

I disagree Life is supposed to be exactly as you decide it to be.

You can choose to see the road ahead smooth, glorious and fun or you can choose to only see the potholes and ups and downs.

They say it is all in the attitude but the attitude feeds on our beliefs, so choose your beliefs carefully. Believe that you can be your true self. Believe that you can be who you want to be. Believe and pass on the same self-confidence to your children.

As Maslow says: "If you deliberately plan on being less than you are capable of being then be sure, you will be unhappy for the rest of your life."

So the happiness we all desire and seem to be in chase of is not somewhere we need to reach or something we need to achieve.

It is about us being in complete alignment with all that we are capable of being. This is a state of happiness.

I have shared all that I learnt in my own personal journey. From a place of need for approval and appreciation, lack of self-love and self-belief to a place of empowered self-worth and unconditional love for my "Self".

My journey of being at the mercy of people around me to feel happy to a place where I know I am in the state of happiness by choice and can remain there as long as I choose to be there.

A journey from questioning my existence to purposeful living. From waiting for years to complete so that I could relieve myself from the misery of life to a place of five years plans for all that I want to accomplish and share with the world.

A journey from silence to finding my voice. A journey of living in hiding to getting out there. A journey of fear to courage.

This has been my journey and I am confident if I can reach here, anyone of you reading this book can too.

All it requires is an awareness and a deep desire to know your true self.

And the journey begins...........

www.ingramcontent.com/pod-product-compliance
Lightning Source LLC
La Vergne TN
LVHW051305200726
843510LV00010B/1284